AMONG
THE NAVAJO

1995-96 NWMS READING BOOKS

RESOURCE BOOK FOR THE LEADER

TOUCHING LIVES THROUGH SHARING
Edited by Beverlee Borbe

FOR THE READER

ARROWS OF THE ALMIGHTY
The Story of William Bromley,
Pioneer Missionary to Papua New Guinea
By A. A. E. Berg

FURLOUGHS, FURLONGS, AND POTLUCK DINNERS
Stories from the Deputation Trail
By A. Brent Cobb

MY LIFE AMONG THE NAVAJO
A Ministry to Body and Soul
By Beulah Campbell

RUN WITH THE TORCH
The Church of the Nazarene in El Salvador
By Eunice Bryant

BRINGING GOD'S WORD TO GUATEMALA
The Life and Work of William and Betty Sedat
By Lorraine O. Schultz

TREASURES IN THE DARKNESS
Stories from Behind Broken Walls
By Sharon R. Martin

My Life Among the Navajo

A Ministry to Body and Soul

Beulah Campbell

Nazarene Publishing House
Kansas City, Missouri

First published 1993 by Bill and Charlotte Clay Enterprises
        and Pro-Ad Communications, Bandung, Indonesia
Reprinted by special arrangement

ISBN 083-411-5581

Printed in the
United States of America

Cover design: Crandall Vail

10   9   8   7   6   5   4   3   2   1

I dedicate this book
to Kathy,
who has been
a silent supporter
since we met in Flagstaff
in February 1956.

Contents

Foreword   11

Acknowledgments   13

1. Becoming "Aunt Boo"   17

2. Gertrude, Low Mountain,
    and Baby No. 1   24

3. A Cold, Lonely Grave   35

4. The Burned Baby   42

5. The Medicine Man   46

6. The Fight   53

7. Slaughtering the Sheep and
    Learning the Language   58

8. Special Deliveries   63

9. Little Jackie Lost   70

Afterword   75

About the Author

Rev. Beulah Campbell was ordained in Denver, Colorado, in 1955 as an elder in the Church of the Nazarene. Within a few months she was assigned to Arizona as missionary nurse to the Navajo at Low Mountain on the Navajo reservation. It was there in Navajoland that she established herself and labored for 30 years. There she and Gertrude Jones (now deceased) founded the Sun Valley Indian School (formerly Twin Wells Indian School) near Holbrook, Arizona. In 1988 a dormitory there was named in her honor.

At present, Beulah is serving as a supply pastor in San Carlos and planning a church plant on the Fort McDowell Indian Reservation just east of Phoenix. Although retired as a missionary, Beulah will not retire from God's service.

Foreword

It's hard to know where you are if you don't know where you've been. That's why we produce NWMS reading books like this one. We tell the stories of the past to be reminded of how far we have come.

Within these pages are a few stories from Rev. Beulah Campbell, a longtime missionary to the Navajo Indians of Arizona. Nina Gunter, general NWMS director, once referred to her as a "Louise Robinson Chapman to the Indians." After reading her stories, I am sure you'll see why.

Most of these stories take place between 1956 and 1970, and they deal with an American culture very different from the one of Ward and June Cleaver, John F. Kennedy, and Woodstock. Yet we must remind ourselves that this too is America, and these too are people for whom Christ died.

The stories you will read in this book were originally related on tape and then transcribed into the form you have before you. Only minimal editing was done to preserve the homespun quality of the stories, so you will read them essentially as Beulah told them. I thought you would enjoy them more that way. So pour yourself a cup of coffee, curl up in your favorite chair, and let Beulah take you on a tour into the fascinating world of the Navajo.

TIM CRUTCHER
NWMS Reading Book Editor

Acknowledgments

I wish to thank the following people for helping me with this book:

Tim Crutcher, for his help in getting this book into its present form;

the Mission Education Committee, for choosing this book for publication;

the Indonesian publisher, Pro-Ad Communications, and Bill and Charlotte Clay Enterprises, for allowing us to reprint the book;

and finally my nephew Bill Clay and his wife, Charlotte, without whose prodding this book would have never come about.

MY LIFE
AMONG
THE NAVAJO

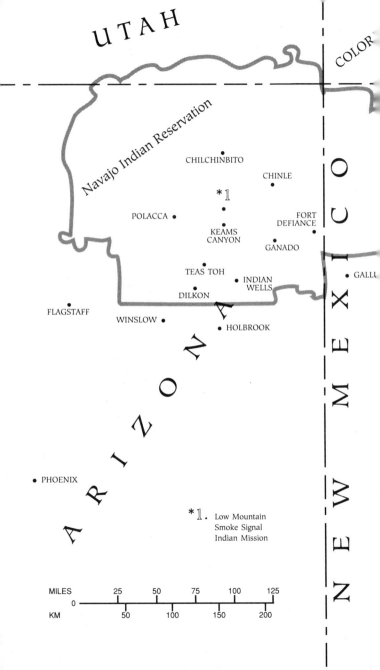

UTAH

COLOR

Navajo Indian Reservation

CHILCHINBITO

CHINLE

*1

POLACCA

FORT
DEFIANCE

KEAMS
CANYON

GANADO

TEAS TOH

INDIAN
WELLS

GALLU

DILKON

FLAGSTAFF

WINSLOW

HOLBROOK

PHOENIX

*1. Low Mountain
Smoke Signal
Indian Mission

MILES   25   50   75   100   125
0

KM   50   100   150   200

A R I Z O N A

N E W   M E X I C O

Becoming "Aunt Boo"

It was December 16, 1955. I had just returned from some pastoral calling when I found the postcard in the mailbox. I was ecstatic. I ran to the house, waving the postcard and shouting, "Here it is! I'm going to the Indians."

As I handed the card to my mother, my brother Lloyd muttered, "I think she is going to the dogs." I wrinkled my nose at him, then leaned over Mom's shoulder as she read aloud:

Sister Campbell,

Your name was sent to me from the Foreign Missions Board for appointment to Low Mountain Mission as a missionary nurse. We need you right away. If you need additional information about the mission, write to Gertrude Jones, Keams Canyon, Arizona.

                    Sincerely,
                    Dr. Swarth
                    District Superintendent
                    North American Indian District

Mom smiled up at me. "Well, that's what you wanted. Good luck."

"Happy birthday," Dad said with a grin.

I was so happy. I got a sheet of paper, sat down beside Mom, and started to write to this Gertrude Jones. I had so many questions: What were the Navajo like? What should I bring? Those kinds of things. I waited a week for the answer to my letter, but I didn't get any information. When a letter finally did come, it read:

Dear Rev. Beulah Campbell,

I've notified Mr. Klineline, who is the pastor at the Nazarene mission in Winslow [Arizona], about your coming. I think it would be good to meet you there before we go out to Low Mountain. Assuming it will take you several weeks to get ready and several more days to get here, we will expect you here on February 8.

I'm very pleased you are coming. Have a nice holiday season.

Gertrude Jones

I couldn't wait to get going. Everyone was glad of my new commission. The Bethel Church, where I had been pastor for the last two years, had a celebration for me. The Yuma, Colorado, Church of the Nazarene, my home church, had a farewell party; and the Yuma Hospital, where I was head nurse, had a "Good Luck" send-off for me. Added to this, the local *Yuma Pioneer* newspaper and the Denver newspapers had articles about me. This notoriety was a little embarrassing, but honestly, it helped me make the break with the family.

At 29, Beulah Campbell is spiritual leader of Bethel Church of the Nazarene, near Yuma, Colo., also is full-time graduate nurse at Yuma Community Hospital.

The picture and accompanying cutline that appeared in the newspaper on the occasion of Beulah's accepting of her call to the Navajo.

Of all these parties, I remember the Bethel Nazarene Christmas party most clearly. We had a Christmas play, and two of my Sunday School pupils, who had been the most mischievous imps I had known, had a bet that one of them would kiss me when I got there. When I arrived at the church, both of these young men ran up and threw their arms around me. One jumped a little higher and planted a big smooch on my cheek. He won the bet. (I didn't know it took a bet to kiss me. I've wondered since, Was I really that bad?)

Having these boys at church in this Christmas play was a wonderful feeling. When I first came to Bethel, these same kids were a constant threat to me, shoving my car behind the privy so I couldn't find it, letting the air out of the tires, and playing many other pranks. They don't know it, but I still cherish that kiss regardless of how much it cost one of them on their bet.

I left Yuma in my '51 Chevy club coupe on February 6 and arrived in Winslow, Arizona, two days later after an overnight in Denver at my sister's and another night at my niece's in Albuquerque, New Mexico. I was eager to get to my first mission with the Navajo, but I took it easy because of the snow—a little hard to do with the anticipation of new, exciting experiences to come.

I looked out the windshield as I slowly drove through the town of Winslow. It was cold and snowing. The snowflakes swirled by a few streetlights to the slushy sidewalks. No one was around. It was getting late in the evening, but I was glad I had arrived at last where I thought was the beginning of a new life.

When I began my studies, I expected that I would be sent as a missionary to some foreign place like Borneo or China. But here I was, right in the middle of the United States. I had studied hard to become an R.N. and subsequently a missionary. I was anxious to do God's will and help His children to know Him. Right now it didn't matter what country. I was here and ready to go to work. What I didn't know but soon learned was that there was an urgent need for care and love awaiting me in the mild and gentle-mannered Navajo people that would be very, very rewarding.

I turned slowly across the slushy street into a service station. I needed direction, and I was getting pretty low on gas. I discovered the Nazarene mission was right in town, only a few blocks away. I paid for the gas, got in the car, and drove back into the slushy street. I pulled into the mission and parked in front of what I figured was the parsonage. I was about to knock when the door swung open to reveal a tall, clean-cut gentleman.

"You must be Beulah Campbell," he said. "Welcome to Arizona. I'm Brother Klineline. Come on in. I really expected you earlier," he said, closing the door behind me. "Were the roads bad?"

"No," I replied. "A little slick here and there, but no real problem. I'm sure glad to be here. Where is Gertrude? I thought she was going to meet me here."

"She had an accident coming down from the mission at Low Mountain and is now in a hospital."

"Oh, my! Is she hurt? I'd like to go see her."

"No, that is not too practical tonight. She is over in Cottonwood near Flagstaff, about 50 miles from here. She suffered a mild concussion when a pickup she was riding in rolled over, but she isn't badly hurt. She should be released by morning, and we'll meet her at the Nazarene mission in Flagstaff.

"Could I get you a cup of coffee?" he continued. "My wife is working this evening at the hospital. She should be home in an hour or two. Do you have some bags in the car I could get for you?"

I sensed that Mr. Klineline was a little nervous with me being there and was trying to make me feel comfortable. On the other hand, I felt a little disappointed not being able to meet Gertrude Jones, the head of our mission at Low Mountain.

We both got up and went to the car for a couple of bags. We sat them in the living room and went back to our coffee. It was only a short time, and we heard a car stop out front. It was almost twelve o'clock, but I was not tired—too eager to find out more about the mission.

Mrs. Klineline and I had a cup of coffee and chatted a bit. "You must be pretty tired from your trip," she said. "I know this has been quite confusing, not knowing what was going to happen next, and for this I apologize. But there is a busy day ahead of you tomorrow, and we've got an early start in the morning." She led the way to a small room. "The room's not much, but the bed is comfy. The bathroom is here, and if you need anything, just holler, OK?"

As she walked away down the cold, narrow hall, I felt warmed by Arizona hospitality. She was a very nice hostess. Things were beginning to look up. I got ready for bed, slipped into the clean sheets, said my prayers as to how I wished to be a good missionary, and drifted off.

I was dreaming of a witch doctor screaming at me when I awoke. Light was streaming in a small window across from my bed as I lay there pondering what missionary life was really like. I was concerned but decided I was ready to go ahead. We had a modest breakfast (I like mush), and we got in the car and headed out to Flagstaff, where I was to meet my boss, Gertrude Jones, the head of our mission.

It took us about an hour to get to Flagstaff. The country was changing from the flat mid-Arizona plains to the higher altitudes. The snow was no longer slush, and the highway was turning to hard ice and compacted snow. Rev. Klineline drove into Flagstaff slowly but confidently. Even so, I was somewhat surprised that we progressed so cautiously. Back in Colorado where I come from, we were accustomed to driving in these conditions. I didn't know then, but my skills in driving in frozen snow like this would hold me in good stead in the years to come.

We drove through Flagstaff, past the downtown shops, and then right a couple of blocks to a cluster of modest, low buildings. "Here we are," announced Mrs. Klineline as we turned into a parking lot.

Two little girls ran out to meet me. One looked barely four, the other about two. "Hi!" said the older one. "My name is Jeanette, and this is my sister, Kathy. We live with Mrs. Jones, and we know you are going to like us. We are going to call you . . ."

"Aunt Beulah," I said.

Little Kathy looked up at me and said, "Boo . . . Boo . . . Aunt Boo-ah."

I picked up Kathy in my arms and said, "Oh my—'Beulah' is too hard. 'Aunt Boo' is just fine."

I liked "Aunt Boo." And so it was, from that first day on the job, I became "Boo" or "Aunt Boo" to almost everyone on the Navajo reservation in Arizona.

Gertrude, Low Mountain, and Baby No. 1

I looked up from the children to see a lady coming out of the mission door to greet me. She stopped and stared. She quickly sized me up and down, just as I was doing to her. After all, we were going to be close partners for many years.

Gertrude Jones was short, about five foot tall. She was wearing an ankle-length flowery dress. She was a little heavy with round facial features: deep-set eyes, soft cheeks, medium nose, and a short neck. There was a warmth in her smile as she looked at me. If, as the saying goes, "Opposites attract," we for sure were that pair. I was much younger, taller, slender, with a long, oval face. I wore my hair in a roll on the back of my head to reveal a high forehead and long neck, which added height to my slender figure.

Wearing a broad grin, I strode forward, saying, "So you're Gertrude Jones. I was beginning to think that we would never meet."

Gertrude *(top left)* and Beulah with Jeanette *(bottom left)* and Kathy in 1960.

To my surprise, she threw her arms around me, although her head hardly came to my chest. "My, I'm glad you're here."

Backing away slightly, I stammered, "I'm glad to be here too."

"Come on inside and we'll talk a bit before we get going," she said.

"Do the two Indian girls, Kathy and Jeanette, belong to this mission?" I was looking around as if their mother might be there.

"No, no," Gertrude explained. "We've adopted them. They are Grace Blackhorse's children. She lives way up north in Chilchinbito. You'll meet her very soon, since you are a registered nurse. She is quite prolific. I think she is already pregnant again. Her small hogan can't accommodate a very large family, but her genes don't understand such things."

After an hour or so of explaining things—more than I could assimilate—Gertrude announced that we'd better get going 'cause there were a number of things to attend to in Winslow before we headed out to Low Mountain, where the mission was.

Gertrude had everything already packed, since she had just come from the hospital. We piled the bags in her pickup. I followed the two girls into the truck, and with Gertrude driving, we followed the Klinelines back to their home in Winslow to spend the night.

I had seen the Klinelines' house, and I couldn't think of how all of us could sleep in such a small space. But missionaries are always resourceful (I soon learned they gotta be), so right after supper Mrs. Klineline gathered up a lot of blankets and made us beds on the floor.

There we were: Gertrude on one end, me on the other end, and the two girls in the middle. Mrs. Klineline knew we were all pretty tired and wouldn't notice the lack of a mattress. She was right. It seemed only minutes and the dawn light was coming through the window, and I was being urged to "shake a tail."

I struggled to my feet and headed for the kitchen.

"Cup of coffee?" Mr. Klineline said.

"Thanks," I said, trying to clear the cobwebs from my head. "I sure conked." After a couple of sips: "I'm getting anxious to see the mission."

"You'll see it soon enough. I sure hope you are not too disappointed," he said.

Too disappointed? I thought. What did he mean by that? I had seen the missions here in Winslow and Flagstaff, and they seemed quite complete, with electricity and bathrooms. What was Low Mountain really like?

It was ten o'clock by the time we had finished breakfast, and I was getting worried that we were not under way. They had told me that the mission was at least a three-hour ride upstate, and at this time of year you couldn't depend on the roads or weather.

Mrs. Jones was already out doing this and doing that, buying groceries and a whole host of things she knew we would need "up there." She knew what it was like but did not want to tell me—for fear that she might lose a supporting missionary, I guess.

We chatted and paced, and I kept looking out of the window to see if Gertrude was there. Finally, shortly after three, there she was in the pickup. It was snowing slightly, but I could see the groceries in the back were covered with a tarp to protect them from the weather. Little did I know, but the "groceries" included nails, boards, cement, and a number of other pieces of maintenance equipment which were needed "out there."

We threw our bags under the tarp and crawled in the pickup. This was it. The Klinelines were not going—just us. I was getting excited. As we drove off, Gertrude said, "Oh, we've got a stop to make before we leave town. We gotta go to the jail."

I looked at her indignantly. "Why? Isn't it getting a little late?"

"It'll only take a minute," she shot back as she dashed out of the truck in front of a low, one-story building and ran inside.

Jeanette, Kathy, and I waited for almost an hour before she reappeared. Walking slightly behind her was a dirty, slovenly dressed Indian. "I knew it," Jeanette said. "She's always getting someone out of trouble. That's Henry Tsossie. He lives up on the reservation near our mission. I bet he was drunk and thrown in the jail. I bet she had to bail him out."

Gertrude came up to the truck and crawled in. "This is Henry Tsossie. He's going to ride back to the reservation with us."

I turned to get a better look at him, but honestly, I was repulsed by his slovenly disposition. He was short and chubby, with a potbelly overlapping his belt. He was dirty, unkempt, shirt open, and in an old jacket. Under his dirty black felt hat his round face was pockmarked and flushed from his previous nights of drinking and carousing.

Even so, I was about to say hello, but he was already in the back of the pickup under the tarp. My acquaintance with Mr. Tsossie would have to wait. As we drove north, Gertrude explained that indeed, Henry had come into town, got drunk, and raised a nuisance. She had paid the bail to get him out, but she said he was a very good man, and it was worth it. "In this work every soul is precious," she added. "You'll see."

From this initiation (and from many later experiences), I was becoming aware that there was no one in this, God's wonderful world, who knew more about drinking Indians and how to handle them than Gertrude Jones.

I smiled as we traveled on. It was dark now, and Gertrude didn't see the grin on my face. We were to go through Holbrook, then out towards Keams Canyon. After about an hour, Gertrude slowed the truck so she wouldn't miss the turnoff. I was watching, too, but when she started to turn, I declare there wasn't anything there but a cow trail headed off across the desert.

"This is it," she exclaimed as if she had discovered some archaeological find. "We go due north from here."

"How much further is it?" I asked. I was tired of this washboard road. The kids were dozing between us.

"Oh, we're almost there. Only 35 or 40 miles more."

Now we were down to a two-lane dirt road. It was half frozen, causing us to slip and yaw as we proceeded. There was no indication that it would ever cease. Each turn only revealed another stretch of nothingness.

What's out here? I wondered. This land wouldn't support gophers, let alone people. On the right we slowly passed one mesa after another. After each bend another mesa appeared. I thought, This one must be it.

But Mrs. Jones said, "Oh no, we have a little further to go."

We rounded another turn, and Gertrude slowed. There on a post was a sign. "Going beyond this point could be dangerous. Travel at your own risk."

"We are now entering the Navajo reservation," she said confidently. At this point Gertrude seemed to relax completely. She was now in Navajoland. She was back with her people. They were kind and humble, except when they had had too much white man's liquor; and she understood them then also.

Believe it or not, that sign didn't bother me either. I seemed already accustomed to this place. In fact, I wouldn't be too surprised to see a witch doctor jump out from one of the rocks and try to frighten me away. If that happened, I fully expected Gertrude, who was an experienced missionary, to speak right out and say, "Boo!" and he would disappear.

We followed that dirty, washboard wagon trail until we came to Indian Wells, where we came to a halt. There in front of us was the mail truck, stuck in a muddy wash. How long he had been there we couldn't tell. Obviously the mail was going to be late today.

Paul Humphrey, the driver, came sloshing over to us and said the most sagacious thing he could think of: "I'm stuck." But miracles exist even out in that forsaken country. Henry Tsossie jumped out of the pickup, and in short order he and Paul had run a line around a scrub tree and managed to get the mail truck out of the wash.

We were next, and with a line on the mail truck across the wash, we were through there and on our way again. I began to realize what Gertrude had said: "In this work every soul is precious. You'll see."

Henry Tsossie jumped into the mail truck with Paul Humphrey, and the two of them drove off into the darkness to Polacca. Again we were alone in the darkness, but we continued on our way. We drove past a number of mesas on our right when finally Gertrude pointed out, "There! There's Low Mountain!"

Silhouetted in the night sky was another mesa, not much different from the dozen or so that we had just passed, but this one I was glad to see. We turned east with the mountain north of us and then north again as we got to the eastern side of Low Mountain. It was a big mountain, and I thought we would never get around it.

We were almost to the mission when a man, a Navajo Indian, stepped out of the brambles and hailed us down. What now? I thought. He started talking Navajo, which was gibberish to me. However, Jeanette alongside of me, only four years old, understood perfectly and told me what he wanted.

"His baby is very near here," she said. "Over under a tree by the wash. He is very afraid that his baby girl will die."

"Why is she out there?" I asked.

"He can't allow her to die in their hogan because, as the medicine man says, Chīndī will inhabit their hogan and cause more misery and death."

I didn't know who Chīndī was, and I didn't dare to ask more questions. This was no time to find out all I didn't know.

31

I told Jeanette to tell him that we would take the baby to our mission and see what we could do for her. (At that moment I didn't know what facilities we had in our mission for taking care of her.) The Indian led me to a scrubby tree nearby and reached down below the branches and pulled out a rough cradle and said, "Here, please take care."

What a frail little thing she was! I took her in my arms, nodded to the man, and walked back to the pickup. "Gertrude, what should we do?"

She motioned me into the pickup, and we drove off. Only a half a mile further, and we pulled into a flat dirt yard; we were at our mission. It was pitch-dark—no lights. I could vaguely see a couple of small buildings: a small house, a small chapel, and a small shed-type building. Gertrude said, "Here we are."

I stepped out onto the frozen yard, staring at the shadowy buildings. My first mission, I thought.

Gertrude motioned to a small house on the left and said, "Take her in there. We will all stay in my house tonight."

A man and a short lady came out of the darkness and welcomed Gertrude and myself. The man immediately started helping with the bags. "We're sure glad you got back OK," he said in Navajo. His wife interpreted the welcome and said, "Here, let me help."

I fed the baby some soup that Gertrude had brought (she thought of everything) and made a bed for her in the corner of the room. I was exhausted. I grabbed some extra blankets, threw them on the floor next to the baby, and crawled in. Neither of us woke till the sun was shining in our eyes. I dressed and walked outside to get a better understanding of our mission.

I looked at Gertrude's house, the little chapel, and across the dirt yard at a shed: the dispensary. Where was the civilization that I left just a couple of hours ago? There were no electric lights, plumbing, central heating, or indoor water faucets. Any resemblance to these comforts was 60 miles away or more. Was I still in the United States?

"Aunt Boo" | dispensary | Gertrude's home | interpreter's home | church | outhouse

A cry from the baby brought me back to reality, and I turned to take care of the problem at hand. My baby was waking up. My first lesson was taking shape: "Take care of the problem in front of you; the rest of them will follow, and most will take care of themselves."

We were both hungry, but she came first. I prepared some warm tea and fed the baby with a spoon even before I changed her. I laid her in the small bed I had prepared for her, and she went fast asleep again.

I relished the moment I had for myself and quickly "showered" (a spit bath) and got myself ready for the duties of the day, whatever they would require. I was ready for my first day in the mission.

I took personal care of that baby, tending to her day and night for almost a week, doing everything except for administering some drugs to her for diarrhea and other drugs to help her stomach disorders. All such medicines were given by Gertrude. I could not officially give them without a doctor's prescription because I was a registered nurse, but Gertrude did not have such a license that could be retracted. She only had an eighth grade education, but she loved her Indians and understood their needs. She also knew how to establish a mission. Gertrude did not worry about administering medicines when they were needed.

When the baby, who we came to know as Nahoni, was well, we took her home to her humble hogan. Her parents and sisters were thrilled to see her. As I was leaving, her father, who had asked our assistance a week earlier, came to me and said something in Navajo.

"What did he say?" I whispered to Gertrude.

"He says you are a powerful doctor," she replied.

I closed my eyes. "Lord, thank You."

As we were driving back to the mission, I thought, Wow! Things sure happen fast around here. I was elated. I leaned back in my seat and glanced over at Gertrude. She smiled back. "There's a lot more to come," she said.

3

A Cold, Lonely Grave

I was finally at the task of putting away the new supply of medicine and ointments in the mission dispensary. It was already getting dark, about eight o'clock, and I was tired. Time for a cup of coffee and bed, I thought.

"Bed" was not far away. I lived in the corner of the dispensary: a separate room with bed and cooking facilities. I even had a toilet, but I had to cover it with a box because it was not connected to anything. The outhouse, 150 feet away, served that item's purpose.

I had just placed the last bottles on the shelf when I heard a galloping horse come to an abrupt stop outside the dispensary door. The rider was a short, stocky man I recognized as a Navajo Indian. I held the lantern up to his face and exclaimed, "Tom! Tom Todecheney—what's wrong?"

Tom had been coming to the mission periodically to help with some of the chores around the place. "Aunt Boo," Tom said pleadingly, "please come at once. My baby is very sick."

I dropped everything and started out the door. I turned back and grabbed my little black case, not knowing what I was getting into. In my three years of experience as a missionary, I already had more weddings and funerals than most of the other denominations in the area. I suspect it was because we were so close and convenient.

As an R.N. at this far-out mission at Low Mountain, I was very busy. Gertrude Jones and I were the only on-site operators, and Gertrude's health had not been good for some time. This left me, as assistant missionary, with all the duties of nurse, teacher, pastor, and chief fixer-upper. Honestly, I enjoyed it.

Tom and Mary Todecheney's place was not far away, about four miles. But with these dirt roads, it would take almost half an hour to get there. By the time I got the pickup turned around and headed around Low Mountain, Tom was already galloping off across the countryside toward his home. How he could run a horse in the dark like that I'll never understand.

I started down the road heading west on the south side of Low Mountain. To call it a road is somewhat of an exaggeration. The land is generally flat below the mesa, so the road is not much more than a wagon track with curves, as required, to circumvent rocks, washes, and ditches. When it thawed, it was a treacherous series of ruts and mud.

But tonight was cold—very cold. A fine snow had fallen, covering the road, providing a falsely smooth path to run on. The steering wheel of the '53 pickup jerked right and left as I bounced from one rut to another. The road gradually turned north on the western side of the mountain.

I had only a mile or so to go, but the driving seemed to take forever. I had sensed the urgency in Tom's voice at the dispensary and was driving as fast as I dared. As I approached the hogan, I noticed that it was typical of the Navajo: octagonal, with 10-foot-long walls on each side, having one room, walls and roof of scrubby four-inch poles with dried mud in between to seal against the elements, and a one-foot hole in the roof to allow the stovepipe from their barrel stove to pass. It was quite low with no windows and could easily be missed or thought to be a large rock in these desolate areas.

When I pulled up to the hogan, Tom was already there. At his feet, just outside the hogan, was a small wrapped bundle. I instinctively knew it was "the very sick baby." I was too late; the baby was already dead.

From Tom, in broken English and Navajo, I found out that the child had died a short while ago. Because he could not afford an official medicine man's "cleansing" ceremony of the hogan, he had placed the boy outside. (To have a death in the hogan meant that the devil was there, and nothing short of burning the hogan down would ensure that he had been driven out.)

Tom asked me if I could take the child, who I knew as Shoni, and bury him that very night near his parents' place across the wash before the medicine man or anyone else knew about the death. I looked up to heaven, closed my eyes, and said, "Lord, Thy will be done."

I picked up the year-old child and very gently placed him on the front seat of the pickup. Tom had held the door open for me. His head was bowed, but there were no tears; Navajo men don't cry. Mary, the mother, had stayed quietly in the hogan, grieving for her lost child.

I started the truck and turned back toward the road. Looking back, I saw Tom stoop, push aside the rug covering the door, and disappear into the hogan. Then I turned the pickup back toward the mission, slipping and sliding in the wagon-wheel ruts. As I drove, I glanced down at the bundle beside me and thought, Boo, you sure have got yourself into some peculiar situations since you came into the ministry of the Lord.

I thought of the time 10 years ago when I approached my parents and said, "Mom, Pop, I've decided to be a missionary."

"Where would you go?" they asked skeptically.

"Oh, I don't know," I replied. "I hear they need missionaries in Borneo."

"Beulah Campbell, I can't let you do that," my father stated flatly. "There are cannibals out there, and they will put you in a pot and eat you."

"You know, Dad, that might be OK. Us Campbells are famous for making good soup."

I chuckled despite myself as I pulled into the mission driveway.

Using the light of the headlights, I got Shoni into the dispensary and decided to tell Gertrude Jones about the situation. Gertrude was always in poor health, and though she couldn't help in this situation, she had to know.

Once Gertrude understood the situation, I took off for Keams Canyon, a small town where there was a government Indian hospital. I knew they would have the boards for a coffin. I also knew I had to bury Shoni that very night to satisfy the family.

By the time I got back to the dispensary, it was already two o'clock in the morning. I packed the boards into the enclosed porch of the dispensary and began hammering and nailing them into a coffin. To an onlooker, the gas lantern hanging from a nail would have revealed an eerie specter indeed: a cloaked figure kneeling over a small, wooden coffin, first nailing it together, then folding an old blanket for padding, and an even older sheet for lining its interior. But no one was watching. I was all alone.

I went into the dispensary, picked up the small body, and laid it gently in the small coffin. With an involuntary shiver I nailed on the top of the box and heaved a sigh. I stood for only a moment, then picked up the box and walked out to the pickup. I wasn't through yet.

Back in the pickup, I drove back west along the south side of Low Mountain. Only a fine snow was falling now; it was even colder than earlier in the evening. The Arizona high plateau country gets real cold in January. The vegetation is so sparse it's a wonder any sheep (or Indians) make it through the winter.

When I reached the western end of the mountain, I turned south off the main road, down across the wash, up the other side, and stopped above Tom's folks' place. Now I had to bury Shoni.

I looked up to the Lord for strength and picked up the box. I had a flashlight, which enabled me to pick my way up a shallow slope to a flat area and set everything down. I propped the flashlight on a rock and started to dig. Beneath about three inches of snow the ground was frozen but sandy. It was a good thing I had thought to bring a pick. It was hard going. Growing up on a poor man's farm in Colorado, followed by three years at this mission, had seasoned me for many tasks, but not this one.

Finally I got down a little more than two feet and thought it enough. I could go no further. I stood for a moment to catch my breath and then picked up little Shoni and put the little coffin into the hole.

I looked up, then down at the grave. "Lord," I said, "in Your infinite love, especially for little children, please take little Shoni and care for him in Your heavenly kingdom."

I hadn't brought my service book, and my mind seemed to be numbing with the cold. ". . . dust to dust, thou shalt return . . . Amen."

I shoveled in the dirt as fast as I could and built a small mound around the grave. In the dim light (I felt the flashlight was about to go out) I quickly placed a ring of rock around the grave. I would return in a day or so to better mark little Shoni's grave.

Not hesitating, I grabbed the pick, shovel, and flashlight and hurried down to the car. The cold was penetrating my cloak. The sweat I had worked up under my clothes was turning icy and was chilling me fast. I stopped at the truck and looked back again at the burial site.

This was the first time I had held a burial service alone. I reached for the door handle. Just then, not far away, came a lonely coyote wail. Maybe I did have a witness after all.

The Burned Baby

It was a beautiful, cold, sunny morning. Now was a good chance to see if I could fix that fence. I just started to push the poles back in place when a young girl came riding up to the mission at a gallop.

"Aunt Boo! Aunt Boo!" she puffed. "My sister has been burned bad. Could you come right away? Please!"

Mable Nutlouis told me in Navajo that her little sister Phyllis had gotten too close to the barrel stove in their hogan because it was so cold, and her dress had caught fire. When she ran out of the hogan, Mable had run after her, threw her to the ground, and patted out the flames, but she was burned very badly.

I ran into the dispensary, grabbed my burn kit, and hollered at my friend, Mrs. Zupke, who was visiting me from Greeley, Colorado. "Come on," I said. "We have an emergency. I may need your help." We ran out, jumped into the pickup, spun around, and headed for the Nutlouis home, not far away.

When we got there, I found that Phyllis's dress had been burned up the back, and her long hair was burned all the way to the top of her head. She was really in bad shape. I cut off the shreds of dress, cleaned the wounds, covered them with burn dressing, and bandaged her with sheet strips that had been provided by the Nazarene Foreign Missionary Society (now Nazarene World Mission Society). Amazingly, the girl did not cry but only winced a time or two as I dressed her.

Phyllis had second- and third-degree burns— there was no time to lose. I told Mrs. Zupke to get in the pickup, and I carefully laid the girl facedown on her lap to prevent abrasion of her wounds. I sure was glad Mrs. Zupke was with me. All the way into Keams Canyon we went as fast as I could drive over that awful washboard dirt road. It was noon before we got to the hospital. As soon as the doctors had looked at her, they rushed her over to Fort Defiance to the Indian hospital.

There wasn't anything more that I or Mrs. Zupke could do, so we climbed in the truck and headed back to Low Mountain. "Is it always like this?" she asked. "How often do things like this happen?"

"Oh, no, not every day," I replied. "Maybe once a month or so. But every incident is different. There are a lot of Navajo out there, and they do have problems. We just happen to be the closest mission with a nurse where they can get help. They really appreciate it.

"Every day we see a few more in church, in school, and helping around the mission—they are very warm people. Before, they only had their medicine man. Now they can also turn to us for help. It takes time and love and patience, but even their medicine man is beginning to respect us."

Realizing she was treading on sensitive ground, Mrs. Zupke said, "I do declare—you missionaries are a different breed of cat."

I drove to the Nutlouis home and explained to them that their daughter was in serious condition but that she was in good care and I believed she would eventually be OK. Mrs. Zupke and I then went back to the mission and had a meal with Gertrude, where we explained the early-morning emergency. The next day Mrs. Zupke took her leave and headed back to civilization.

I went back into the dispensary and started to restock my burn kit. I walked to the door and looked out at our chapel, the little house where Gertrude lived, and across the barren landscape still covered with a dusting of snow.

This is a lonely place, but isn't it beautiful? I felt glad that I was the one to help that little girl. Being a missionary isn't all that bad.

The next day, and frequently for several weeks, I drove into Fort Defiance to see Phyllis. Burns heal slowly. Every week or so there was additional surgery. She was in the hospital so long that everyone knew her and admired her spunk.

One day a doctor came up to me and said, "Aunt Boo—may I call you Aunt Boo like all the Indians do?—well, that little gal sure knows how to pray. You must have taught her a lot of the Bible in your Sunday School. She never would have made it with all the infection she had if she didn't have so much faith in Jesus."

"Thank you, doctor, and all your staff for everything you've done for her." I quickly turned and walked down the hall to prevent my tears from showing. My thoughts went back to the Bible: "And whoso shall receive one such little child in my name receiveth me" (Matt. 18:5).

I kept track of Phyllis over the years. When you see her, you would never know how seriously she had been burned. She learned how to do her hair and how to dress so all of her scars were covered. She graduated from college and now teaches school over in Chinle.

Life is like that. The results of a kindness often take years to bloom.

The Medicine Man

It was early; the sun was just coming up. I was awake but stayed snuggled in the covers because it was so cold. It had snowed that night, but now the skies were clear, the full moon fading in the morning light.

I heard a pickup coming down the road, so I popped out of bed and quickly dressed. The truck drove right up to the fence in front of the dispensary. Raymond Gene, who owned the only other pickup in the area (one with a broken muffler), had come from a medicine camp a few miles away, where his father, Frank Cowboy, the chief medicine man, had been singing over a young woman for several days.

Raymond said, "The medicine man told me to get the new 'Azee ił inīī nez' and bring her as soon as possible. Can you come?" (I was the new "tall medicine maker.")

"Of course," I told him. "I have a couple of things to get ready, but I will come right away."

He spun his pickup around and was gone. Raymond did not like being a messenger between his father and me.

I walked back into the dispensary with my interpreter, Gladys, and out of curiosity I asked her if she had ever seen a ritual done by a medicine man over a sick girl.

At first she hesitated, like maybe there could be some repercussions if the medicine man ever found out. But as I packed my little black bag, she said, "My father was a medicine man."

I was shocked. I had been with Gladys Johnson for over a year, and I didn't even suspect.

"I was only 13 years old," she continued, "when I saw my first and only ritual by my father. He was trying to cure a pain in a young girl's left side, about here." She pointed just below her heart. "It could have been a gallstone or some small tumor, but it was giving the girl a lot of pain.

"First my father made an herb concoction of a number of different kinds of roots, leaves, and berries. This he brewed for several hours before giving it to his patient. She drank it very slowly, gagging several times, and pushed the remainder away.

"Next, he took a large number of 'special' stones from a sack and made a circle with them around the girl. A circle means one or unity and is to define a line around the patient for the spirits to enter or leave. The ritual is to be performed under a clear sky so the spirits can find their way easily. Cloudy skies confuse spirits.

"Then my father prayed (chanted) over the girl for a long time—several hours without interruption—after which he slumped down, exhausted, and rested quietly for an hour or so.

"My father then took a root from a basket beside him and started to chew it vigorously. It must have been very hot, because beads of sweat broke out on his forehead, and his face turned very red. He took the mashed root from his mouth and pressed it over the painful area under the girl's heart. After several minutes he placed the root back in his mouth, chewed it, and spit it into the glowing fire. The fire flared several feet in the air and subsided."

I was ready to depart, but I didn't want Gladys to stop. "Go on," I said. "What else did he do?"

"My father took a different root," she said, "and chewed it and placed it on the girl's chest. After several minutes, he removed it, put it back in his mouth, and spit into the fire. He did this several more times. Each time the flames shot up.

"My father next took some remaining mash from his mouth and, after massaging it, pressed it to the girl's skin directly over the pained area with his hand. He worked it in and out until the skin was quite discolored. He molded the pulp from her body with his hand and flung it to the fire, causing another violent flare.

"My father was completely exhausted and collapsed forward over the body of the girl and laid there for several minutes. Soon he straightened up and sat rigid, staring into the fire. He sat with her like that all night. The next morning the girl opened her eyes, got up, and walked out of the medicine man's tent to her own hogan. She was apparently cured."

I didn't want to believe the story, but I knew Gladys was relating it just as it happened. "Is there more?" I asked, heading for the door.

"My father was exhausted. He staggered to his tent and collapsed. The next day he emerged from his tent and went for a short walk, singing to the morning sun and the birds along the way. The next day was a similar routine—only he walked further and sang louder. The third day he talked to members of the tribe. I do not understand or know more than I've told you."

I stood entranced by her story but knew we should have been on our way long ago. "Thank you, Gladys," I said, "but please don't tell anyone that you told me all this." I turned and left for the medicine man's camp.

Mrs. Jones was waiting for me by the pickup, so I jumped in and headed down across the valley from the mountain. "Why do we do this for the medicine man when he and his kind are always trying to chase us out of here?" I asked Gertrude. "Just a week ago an Indian was on the roof of my dispensary, banging and shouting that his ancestors lived here and this was their ground."

"We will get a lot of haranguing to try our strength," Gertrude replied, "but in the end they want us. You'll see." Gertrude was always very positive. "We should always come when they call us. Eventually they will thank us. You'll see."

We started down through a dry wash, and there we stopped. To my embarrassment I found the truck was out of gas. I knew that this was not unusual—for Gertrude to run out of gas. We were always watching pennies, but out here we needed transportation. Never again, I resolved.

It was midmorning and the ground was still frozen, so we decided to walk. We left the pickup and started down the road. We knew the school bus would be along soon. They would either pick us up or go get some gas to get us going again.

We had no idea how far the medicine man's camp was, but we were going to give it a try. I had on my boots and Gertrude had hers. We were dressed for the cold morning but not prepared for the thawing midmorning slush. We walked in the snow and mud for miles. We were near exhaustion. We thought we would never run out of turns in the road.

Frank Cowboy

We finally rounded another mesa and saw the Nelson camp, where Frank Cowboy, the medicine man, had been singing over the sick woman. They were expecting us and were already cleaning away the paraphernalia used by the medicine man. I was held off until they could get the patient ready for my examination, which I did immediately.

After a little while, I diagnosed that this woman was suffering from an ectopic pregnancy: a life-threatening pregnancy wherein a fertilized egg implants itself in the fallopian tube rather than the uterus. As the embryo develops, the tube grows beyond its capacity, causing pain and hemorrhaging. This was a serious situation.

I talked to the medicine man through an interpreter and after a very long time got permission to take her to a hospital because I knew she needed surgery immediately. We now had to wait until the ground froze again, because the road to the hospital was nearly impassable. This meant spending the rest of the day waiting.

The school bus had already come. It had brought the kids home from school and had left again to get gas for our vehicle. I was anxious, but I tried to relax and keep the patient as comfortable as possible.

In the meantime, the Navajo had made dinner for us and everyone else in the camp—a large pot of stew. We all knelt down around this big pot in the middle of the floor. I sat on the most beautiful rug I'd ever seen. I looked into the pot, and there was a sheep's head peeking out at me. The eyes and grinning teeth were looking right at me, as if I was responsible for its predicament. The Navajo had made the mutton stew and had cooked the entire carcass in it.

I watched the Navajo dig in. I noticed that as each of them took their dry fry bread and dipped in the stew, every hand came out cleaner than it went in. This was my first experience with home-made Navajo stew. Having no alternative, I decided to go ahead—it surely couldn't kill me just this once. I reached in the pot with my bread and slowly turned the sheep's head toward the medicine man. He looked at me and slowly turned the sheep's head toward Gertrude. I smiled at her, raised my eyebrows, and dipped in. Life with the Navajo is a matter of faith and understanding.

I'll never forget that first mutton stew: it was delicious. Many times since, I've had mutton stew in hogans with the Navajo. It goes with the territory, and it is always good.

That afternoon we took the woman all the way to Ganado, where there was a Presbyterian hospital. There they did surgery that very night. Yes, she had an ectopic pregnancy. We saved her life.

"Thank You, Lord."

6

The Fight

It was Saturday evening. Gertrude and I were sitting in front of her little house discussing the possibilities for tomorrow's sermon. "Gertrude, isn't it the children who we should emphasize, for they 'shall inherit the earth'?"

"But we are all children in God's eyes," she said. Gertrude had an inner sense about the Navajo. "Underneath that rough exterior, which we help create, is a warm human being waiting to be found."

I wanted to interject something about saving those who would shape the future, but just then a girl came riding up and stopped my train of thought. "Joe Martínez is going to kill Uncle John!" she gasped. "He's drunk and crazy. Can you do something? Quick!" she pleaded.

"Get the truck," Gertrude ordered as she ran into the house. "I'll be right with you."

I reeled the pickup around the yard, stopped long enough for Gertrude to jump in, and sped down the road. The girl was about a quarter mile ahead of us; it was only a few miles to the Martínez place.

As we bounced along the road, Gertrude explained that Joe had been away, working on a railroad, and that John, his uncle, had become a Christian and sworn off booze. She suspected that Joe wanted to celebrate and John would not have anything to do with it.

I looked across at Gertrude, who was checking a very large revolver to see that it was loaded and armed. What was she going to do? Kill Joe? I had never seen such a big pistol. "I just keep it around in case of an emergency like this," she explained. "I hope we are not too late."

"Well, I never," I said and stepped on the gas.

We got to the Martínez place in about 15 minutes. There was Joe chasing John with an ax. John was running for his life.

I went to John and said, "This way." Gertrude went after Joe. "Boom!" the gun went off as Gertrude fired the cannon into the air.

Joe came to a screeching halt, turned to Gertrude, and shouted, "Go ahead! Shoot! I could do thish good even ish my eyesh were closed."

Before Joe could recover as to what was going on, I had gotten John into the pickup and was headed out. Gertrude turned and jumped aboard just as we pulled away.

When we got back to the mission, I grabbed John and rushed him into the dispensary. I pushed John into a corner, covered him with blankets, pulled the drapes on the windows, and pushed the bed against the door. Gertrude had stayed at the pickup with the gun, because we did not know for sure what was going to happen.

I peeped out the window, and there was Joe, galloping into the mission. I watched Gertrude talk to him by the truck for at least 20 minutes. All the time Joe was ranting and waving his arms.

Gradually his animation diminished, and Gertrude led him by the arm into her little house. What was happening now?

John whispered from his hiding place, "What's going on?"

"I don't know," I said. "I'll go see. You stay put."

I walked across the yard separating Gertrude's house and our dispensary and peeked into her kitchen. There was Joe, on his knees, humbling himself before Gertrude, obviously asking forgiveness from her and God. I quickly retreated to the dispensary and told John that I thought the trouble was over. John waited until Joe had left, and then we went to talk with Gertrude.

"Oh, Joe?" she said. "He's just fine. He's a very fine boy. He'll be back for church in the morning. One of these days he'll be one of our Sunday School teachers. He wants to do something constructive." She smiled. "We will train him and give him the chance."

That little missionary, Gertrude, really had a way with her Navajo. She loved them, and they loved her too. I drove off to take John back to his home. "All I can say is—she is the closest thing to a saint that I've ever seen," I told him.

John nodded. "I agree, and I'm really glad she is." We looked knowingly at each other.

What was she saying this morning? I pondered as I drove back to the mission. We are all children in God's eyes. How things have changed! I thought, not realizing that it was me who had changed since I had left my home in Yuma, Colorado. Fights, but mostly their results, do change our futures.

I drove back toward our mission, my mind jumping back to when I had my first bout with my brother Lloyd back on the farm. We were on our way to school when he decided that he was not going to school anymore. He was in the eighth grade, and that was as far as he was going to go. All he wanted out of school was to play football, and football season was over.

I was younger than Lloyd but was determined to get my education no matter how difficult it was for me. I needed him for my transportation to school and back. For him to abandon me and leave me without an education was unacceptable.

I argued that it wasn't fair, and the next thing I knew, he had stopped the car on the gravel country road, and we were out there on the side of the road having a real fistfight. I was determined to go on with my education, and Lloyd seemed determined to stop me.

Well, as most fights go, we soon forgot what we were fighting about and quit swinging at each other. He did quit school, however, so I started to ride my dad's horses to school every day. At the time it didn't seem too much to get up at daybreak and ride six miles to my high school in Otis, Colorado, and then ride back to our house in the evening.

One horse, Major, wasn't too bad, but old Silver went up and down as much as he went forward. No matter how many times I took that trip, my bottom always ended up sore. Fortunately, I worked a schedule where I only rode Silver twice a week. In this way I survived, and I got my education the hard way. And God used those experiences to prepare me for the early mornings and bumpy roads I faced every day in Navajoland.

I pulled into the mission and walked over to Gertrude, who was waiting for me. "John's OK for now. I sure have to hand it to you for pulling that one out of the fire, Gertrude."

"We are all little children," she said. "I think that will be a good subject for your sermon tomorrow."

Slaughtering the Sheep and Learning the Language

I stood in the dirt yard between the chapel and the dispensary. I looked south across the valley toward the mesa where Jane Begay lived. It was six o'clock in the morning and two hours before Sunday service. I fully expected Jane to come, but at the moment she was nowhere in sight. She was either sick or off schedule.

Gertrude knew my concern and waved at me as I sped out of the mission and headed south down the road. My worries that something had happened to her were unfounded, however. When I got to the other side of the valley, there was Jane, headed for church, crawling down the road in front of me.

Jane could not walk; she had to crawl wherever she went. She had started early, and I had missed her when I first looked up on the south mesa. She was already at the bottom of the hill.

58

I stopped alongside of her. She smiled a greeting and crawled into the back of the pickup; the springs sagged appreciably. Jane was very heavy from her sedentary life, but she was very strong and could crawl or climb almost anywhere.

Normally, Jane Begay tried to get to our church every Sunday by herself. She would crawl down the hill and across the valley to our mission (approximately four miles) on her hands and knees. She got there early and left late to keep others from giving her sympathy. I usually tried to pick her up and always took her home. We were as discreet about it as possible. Everyone knew, but no one let on about Jane's handicap as they visited her in church.

Jane had been crippled for as long as anyone could remember. Some thought it was from birth, and others thought it was from some early disease. One thing was for sure—Jane Begay could not walk.

Today she had been earlier than usual because she had wanted to talk to me. "Aunt Boo," she said after getting settled in the pickup, "would you help me butcher a young sheep?"

I knew better than to ask her why her husband didn't help her. I had helped my folks butcher cows and hogs and what have you when I was growing up, so I thought I knew enough about it to help. (I really thought that it wasn't just help she wanted: I was to do the whole thing.)

"When do you want to . . . ah . . . kill your sheep?" I asked as I helped her out of the truck at the mission. I was not sure this was what I wanted to get into.

"Could we do it right away? Could we do it this afternoon?" she asked.

I helped her into a pew at the back of the church. Nobody was around yet and wouldn't be for an hour or so. She bowed her head and started to pray. I put my hand on her shoulder for a moment and said, "Sure," not relishing what I was getting in for. "Mrs. Jones will take you home after the service, and I'll be up there about three o'clock. OK?" Jane smiled appreciatively. She knew that I'd come.

That afternoon I drove the pickup slowly up the rugged mountainside road to her very modest hogan. She had already made one trip to the spring for a bucket of water. I picked up two buckets she was struggling with and carried them back to be heated so that we would have ample hot water for the butchering.

A young sheep, bleating noisily, was tied in a small pen next to the hogan. About 50 feet away was a shallow pit waiting for the innards and waste. Someone, probably her husband, had brought the sheep in, dug the hole, and then left on other business—not too surprising.

The water was hot, and there were several additional pots of water ready for cleaning. I picked up a large mallet and headed for the hapless sheep.

I will spare you the details of the butchering, but it went rather quickly. Within an hour we had the meat laying on a large sheet of butcher paper, and Jane was wrapping various cuts to keep the flies off and make ready for immediate smoking and preservation.

Jane also had a large stew going in the hogan and was throwing all the meat fragments into the pot. This aroma was having an effect on my appetite as well as her husband's, Fatty Begay, who mysteriously appeared, coming down the path. He said the sheep in the south side of the mesa were OK and that he had just come by to see how we were doing.

I knew this was malarkey, but that was Fatty's way, and I was not going to change it in my lifetime. He would come around after the work was done. Jane did most, if not all, of the menial work.

We were soon all settled around a pot of stew in the middle of their hogan and were about to dip in. The upper part of Fatty's shirt was unbuttoned, and his belly was hanging over his belt. You might politely say that his chest had fallen. The Navajo do not wait for a blessing, so I interjected a compliment to Fatty as soon as I could. "Gohwēēh dōtōōō ahayōī, hastīīn," I said. ("Too much good coffee, man.")

To my surprise, everyone laughed. They thought I had said, "Awēē dōtōōō ahayōī, hastīīn." ("Too many babies, man.")

That evening, as I left the Begay hogan and headed down to the mission, I resolved that I had to take a course in the Navajo language. How many times had I been misunderstood? It should not be necessary that they learn English to understand me. I should know Navajo to understand them. I thought if I tried to speak to them in their language, they would have more respect for me.

I studied hard and thought that I had progressed sufficiently in my elocution of their language to be able to use it in one of my sermons. So one Sunday I said in my best Navajo, "You know, if we were skinned, we would all be alike."

An elderly Navajo lady raised her hand and said, "No, no—backwards you talk."

She was right. The Navajo reverse their sentences: "To town going I am." I should have said, "If alike, we would all be skinned."

I remembered an Indian phrase, "You must walk a full moon in your fellow brave's moccasins before you judge him." It's an old Indian saying, but I was beginning to appreciate it more each day. It would take language and a lot of time before they would fully understand me and I would fully appreciate them.

8

Special Deliveries

As I've said, every day is a new adventure at the Low Mountain Indian Mission. Small as it was, being that far north into the Navajo reservation, we were usually involved in all of their everyday problems. In fact, it sometimes seemed the Navajo went out of their way to be sure we were involved.

It was a spring morning: the air was fresh, the snow was gone, and everywhere there seemed to be new life stirring. Jeanette and Kathy were playing some sort of hopscotch in the yard and were having a great time.

I looked up from the job of bracing the fence around the dispensary as a pickup came noisily into the yard. (I don't believe the Navajo have heard about muffler replacements yet.) Grace Blackhorse slid out of the right side of the truck in time to embrace her two children. After the excitement of the renewed visit, Grace came over to me and said, "Would you please deliver my new baby?"

I did not ask her when it was due; her stomach indicated that it could be any time. I explained to Grace that I wasn't allowed to deliver babies. If I did, I would be acting the part of the doctor, and that was forbidden. I was just a registered nurse and should only assist during childbirth. However, I told Grace that if the baby started to come on our way to the hospital, I felt the government would stand behind me if I had to do something.

Grace understood. We decided that she would stay there in the dispensary a few days until the baby was due, and then we would go to the hospital in Keams Canyon as fast as we could. She liked the arrangement and settled down in the dispensary just outside the door to my cubicle. Grace understood that as soon as she started having labor pains, she would tell me and we would start for the hospital.

Things were quite uneventful for about two weeks. We all expected the baby anytime, but nothing happened. Then about two o'clock one morning (why does everything happen at night?) Grace hollered at me from the other side of the door in the dispensary that she was having labor pains. Grace couldn't speak English, but I knew enough Navajo to understand what was happening.

I jumped out of bed, dressed, and ran over to our interpreter's little house to ask them to go to the hospital with us. Bob and Allison Pokegan, newlyweds, were acting as our interpreters in the mission at this time. I tapped loudly on the window of their house and shouted, "Grace's water has broke."

Allison understood me and knew that we would be taking Grace to the Indian hospital. Bob, however, who knew nothing about having babies, jumped out of bed, dressed, and left immediately to shut off the water pipes up at the spring.

When I drove back by their house to pick up my interpreters, Allison was laughing so hard about Bob trying to shut off Grace's water up at the spring that she could hardly tell us what had happened. All the way driving into Keams Canyon Hospital, it seemed that every time Grace would have a pain, we would all start laughing again about Bob.

When we drove up to the hospital, there were nurses waiting for us, and they immediately rushed Grace inside. Within minutes, it seemed, baby Leonard was born, a fine, healthy boy.

I recently visited him in Flagstaff. He is married now with a child of his own and another on the way. For some reason he couldn't remember that night 30 years ago when I first met him!

Oh yes, Mother Grace is still doing well. Like many Navajo women, she spends her time making rugs and blankets for her family and a few to sell to the tourists. At last count she had produced approximately 25 rugs, 15 blankets, and 11 beautiful children. Yes, the 11 children is also an approximate number.

Grace Blackhorse and one of her latest blankets

About a week after this pregnancy, I received a message from the Foreign Missions Board of the Church of the Nazarene to say that they believed I was ready for an appointment overseas. I had asked for this opportunity back in college, but the situation today was entirely different.

I jotted down a letter to them, saying that I was very happy with the Navajo, that they were a very warm and wonderful people. I do not know how many of my superiors they consulted, but I did not hear of any future potential callings to far-off Borneo or the equivalent.

I do believe that my friends, Indians and whites alike, appreciate that I was, for some divine reason, destined to be here in Navajoland to administer my services to my friends. I loved this land and these people just as Gertrude did.

Sometime later I was enjoying a warm evening in May, unwinding from the busy Sunday schedule. I was talking to Gertrude about the coming week of festivities in Keams Canyon, where the Navajo were having an open fair to show off their rugs and pottery to the local merchants. Some of the tourists were already gathering to partake in the summer activities. Everyone knew the best buys would come early and would gradually diminish as the available stock diminished. It would be a gala fair, and we all wanted to be helpful to our local Navajo community.

For a change, things were quiet here on the Navajo Nation. Gertrude and I thought that we could relax and enjoy their activities without any great effort on our part. However, down the road into the mission courtyard came a pickup, spinning around to a dusty halt in front of the dispensary, where we were sitting.

"Good night," I muttered. "What now?"

I looked at Gertrude to see her wagging her head side to side to express, "Who knows?"

Out jumps the chief's son, Desert Storm, and shouts, "My wife is having her baby! We must get her to a hospital quickly!"

I looked at Gertrude, raised my eyebrows, and headed for the dispensary. Is there no peace in Navajoland? I thought. I came running with my black bag and shouted an order at Desert Storm to stay there and we would get his wife to the hospital. His wife jumped from the pickup to our jeep, and away we went.

I figured that if we took the road due south to Keams Canyon and then east to Ganado, it would take at least an hour. We did not have that much time. However, by cutting diagonally southeast across the pastureland, we could save 15 minutes. After all, the jeep with four-wheel drive could go anywhere, right? Furthermore, the road across the pasture was not much worse than the country road with its chuckholes, washboard surface, and dangerous washouts on turns due to rain and poor maintenance. I had to take the chance.

Away we went, and a jostling time we had. Part of the way it seemed we were making good progress. Desert Storm's wife in the backseat advised that the contractions were coming very fast and that the baby was coming very soon. I pushed the throttle a little harder and tried to hold the jeep steady, but it swirled to the side and came to a soft stop in a sand drift.

I gunned all wheels, but the jeep refused to budge from its present position. I was stuck. I was halfway to Ganado, but the jeep would go no further at this moment.

I looked back at the lady and reached for the flashlight. The light came on very dim. Her time had come, and the batteries were almost gone. I would have to hurry.

Fifteen minutes later, I presented a little boy to her, whom she later called Jason Yellowhair. The baby was in fine shape. I cleaned him the best I could and wrapped him in the blankets we had. The mother cuddled the baby to her and fell asleep from exhaustion.

I picked up a shovel from the back of the jeep and started to shovel the sand away from the wheels. After about 15 minutes, I tenderly prodded the jeep into action, and we moved out of the sand trap and across the pasture toward Ganado. When we finally got to the hospital, about an hour later, the nurse on duty took over and made the mother and the baby comfortable for the night.

Today Jason Yellowhair is a responsible leader of the Navajo Nation. Yes, he knows me, but he doesn't remember that night in the jeep. But who does remember that person who first welcomes him into this world?

Little Jackie Lost

I bounced up and down and side to side as I drove the pickup north back to Smoke Signal Indian Mission, the new name of our mission on the base of Low Mountain. In the valley between our mesa and the next one to the south of us, the smoke from the Indian hogans often went straight up, leaving long, thin trails in the sky. On calm days, little gusts of air broke up the columns into puffs of smoke like smoke signals. So we adopted that as the name for our mission.

The ground was frozen, causing the steering wheel to jerk as the wheels slid through the hard ruts. It was a cold, clear, beautiful evening. The golden sky, streaked with red, wispy clouds, silhouetted the desert mesas and rock formations, forming scenes that would challenge any artist. This was becoming my land, "Beulah Land," that biblical space and time just this side of heaven. I took my time letting the steering wheel guide itself through the ruts like an old horse plodding home.

I was awakened from my reverie by a man on a horse coming down the road toward me. As I came to a stop, I recognized him as Jason Judy, a young lad from the north side of the mountain. "Aunt Boo, Jackie Geneha is lost on Low Mountain. He went up there this morning with his grandpa to keep him company. His gramps [who was Frank Cowboy, the medicine man] somehow let Jackie stray away while he was tending the sheep."

"Well, what is happening now?" I asked. "Is he still up there? What can I do to help?" It was already dark, and the night was getting colder. That mesa was no place for a little boy to be tonight.

"Jackie is still lost, I guess, at least he was when I left about an hour ago. Frank Cowboy asked me to come and get you to see if you could come up there. When Frank couldn't find the boy right away, he lit a fire and sent up smoke signals calling for help. Half the men in the area are up there right now, looking all over for him. Frank doesn't want you to search but would like you to come to the top in case they need a nurse when they find Jackie."

"Well, of course I'll come," I said. "The mission is just ahead. I'll go get my bag and some blankets, and I'll start right up. Jason, why don't you come to the mission and ride with me and tell me all about it? You can leave your horse there or tie him to the truck."

Within 15 minutes, I was headed up the mountain with Jason beside me, his horse on a long

71

lead tied behind the pickup. Jason was telling me that there wasn't much snow up there, but it was very cold. "All Jackie had on at noon today when he strayed off was a skimpy T-shirt. The sun was warm enough at noon, so that he didn't need a coat. The searching parties didn't get formed till late this afternoon when the men arrived. Do you think he'll be all right, Aunt Boo?"

"The mountain is only so big, and with all those men I'm sure they'll find him," I said. What I was really worried about was the possibility that Jackie had fallen into a hole or ravine and was badly hurt. That and the cold could be very serious.

We were on top now, and Jason directed me to a little hogan that Frank used while tending his sheep. I shut off the pickup, and from all over the mesa came the strains of an Indian chant as the men sang while searching for Jackie.

There were several men standing close to the hogan, listening to the searchers to determine if there were any new developments. One motioned me inside. It was a very small hogan with a low fire in the barrel in the middle of the room, but it was warm, for which I was very grateful. I sat on the floor and listened to the eerie chanting in the distance. I bowed my head and prayed that Jackie would be found safe and sound.

It must have been well after midnight when I became aware that the chant was growing louder and nearer. It was now a cheery song. I was getting up to see why the change, and in walked

Frank Cowboy carrying little Jackie in his arms. "We were clear across the top of the mountain when we heard him crying," he said. "He had fallen on a thistle cactus and couldn't get up. It was a good thing he was crying, or we might not have found him so soon. He seems OK, but would you check his bottom for needles and scratches?"

Frank handed little Jackie to me and went outside with the other men. I unwrapped the blanket and checked him over. He didn't have any serious injuries except for a few scratches, to which I applied a little ointment to ease the pain. I wrapped Jackie in the blanket again and took him outside to his grandfather.

I was about to beg my leave and head back to the mission when the medicine man said, "Aunt Boo, we all have thanked our gods for helping us find Jackie safe. Now we want to bow our heads while you thank your God for his safe return."

I stepped back to gain my composure and prayed, "Heavenly Father, thank You for Jackie's return, and bless all these dedicated men who helped in the search until he was found. Amen."

I nodded my farewell and crawled in the pickup. As I drove away, I was overwhelmed, and tears came to my eyes. This experience awakened in me the fact that there were still many souls out there who needed to be found, and we in the ministry should continue to seek until we find each of them. Occasionally, each of us are like lost sheep who have gone astray. And each of us at times needs someone to help us find our way home again.

It was morning twilight by the time I got back to Smoke Signal Mission. I was so absorbed in my thoughts that I hadn't noticed a rider loping behind me. He pulled up to the side of my pickup just as I was about to turn into the mission yard. I stopped just as he did. It was Frank Cowboy, the medicine man. He was the last Indian I would have expected here at the mission.

"You forgot your medicine bag," he stated firmly. "We may need it again." He thrust the black bag into the window of the pickup. We looked at each other for a moment with a deep understanding that I'll never forget. Then with a straight back, he reined his horse and trotted back down the road behind me.

I pulled into the mission to see Gertrude outside her little house, smiling at me. She had seen Frank Cowboy deliver the bag, and I'm sure she liked what she saw.

It had been a long night, but at this moment I was not a bit tired. I was very happy as I walked to the dispensary. I liked being a missionary nurse in Navajoland.

Afterword

It has been almost 40 years since I became a missionary among the Navajo and met Gertrude, Kathy, Jeanette, Frank Cowboy, and all those others. Much has changed since then. Little Kathy is now married and has two children. She and I are still wonderful friends, but few others are left from our original crew. We lost Jeanette and her little son during a difficult delivery back in 1976. Gertrude passed on to her reward after a long illness in 1979. She had been a wonderful pioneer missionary, and it was a joy to have worked with her.

(Above right) "Aunt Boo" today with Kathy and her husband, Gene Taylor, and their sons, Kevin (left) and Jason.

Still, as these have passed on, there have been others who have arisen to take their places. One example of this is the pastor of the Nazarene church in Teas Toh, Dennis Johnson, who is the son of Gladys Johnson, my interpreter. His wife is a schoolteacher in Dilkon and also serves as the district treasurer.

Other changes besides personal ones have also taken place over the years. Even before I left Smoke Signal on the Navajo reservation, dispensing of medications was being challenged as illegal for a missionary nurse. The transporting of patients to clinics or hospitals was beginning to be the task of relatives or friends who had transportation. The Indians come into town more and do many tasks for themselves that were once done by missionaries.

Still, the work of spreading the gospel continues, and now that is being done more and more by the Indian people themselves. When D. Swarth was the district superintendent of the Indian work, there was a strong feeling that to build a Church of the Nazarene among the people, a Bible school was a necessity. Such a school was born at Lindreth, New Mexico. It fought for existence in the beginning years and almost became extinct in that far-out area. But with careful vision for the need and possibilities, the school was moved to Albuquerque, New Mexico. In its early days, Native American boys and girls were admitted to elementary grades through high school. Brother Swarth, Rev. Charles Scribner, Rev. G. H. Pearson, Rev. Merle Gray, and many others carried heavy burdens during these years. It has struggled, but it has survived.

Today, that school, Nazarene Indian Bible College (NIBC), is working to train leaders and workers for the Indian church. It is accredited under our Nazarene Bible College and operates under the leadership of R. T. Bolerjack. The school has also expanded its work to include new programs in office management and human services, as well as discipleship and evangelism. Twelve new buildings have been built in the last 10 years.

NIBC has produced some very well-equipped graduates. Among them are Johnny Nells, our district superintendent on the Navajo Nation District (which was created in 1985 and encompasses the Navajo Indian Reservation), and Rev. Julian Gunn, who served 20 years as our district superintendent on the Southwest Indian District (formerly the North American Indian District).

Back in Arizona, we too were feeling the need to educate our people, though we were thinking in terms of a grade school. In 1963 Gertrude and I were involved in the purchase of land in Sun Valley, Arizona, where we began the Twin Wells Indian School (now Sun Valley Indian School). We began with 7 little girls, but that number grew to 56 in just two years. Today the school has an enrollment of 146 and operates under an independent board, but it is still tied to the Church of the Nazarene.

In 1975 the responsibility for the work among the Indians was transferred from the Foreign Missions Board to the Home Missions Department, now the Church Growth Division, through which the work receives support from the General Budget. Today there are 35 churches on the two districts and 5 church-type missions. And the work continues to grow as we work to plant new churches and expand existing work.

Work teams from outside the district have played an important role in building the church (literally) in the past years. Many Work and Witness teams from across North America have given of their time and money to build church buildings, parsonages, and other structures. Each year, hundreds of high school students from California take part in the Y.E.S. (Youth Equipped to Serve) Projects sponsored by Point Loma Nazarene College. These young people have painted and fixed up many of the older buildings across the district and have taken part in other large-scale construction projects.

Worship among our Indian brothers and sisters is alive and exciting. We have an exciting group of young people at our district camps and conferences, and they can sing the glory down. Attending one of their prayer services, one can feel the glory of the Lord. The testimonies of salvation and sanctification, the messages they bring on holiness of heart, the Christlikeness in their activities can all leave one with assurance that the Holy Spirit is at work through the Church of the Nazarene among our North American Indians of the Navajo Nation and Southwest Indian districts.

There are many good things happening among the Indian people of the Southwest, but they still need our prayers. Many of our smaller churches struggle to meet expenses, just as they do elsewhere. The problem of alcoholism is a real one, and there are many who struggle with it.

We need to pray the Lord of the harvest to send more workers into the harvest. Even at our district assemblies, it seems the older people are the burden bearers. Often young people will graduate, find a good government or local job, and become busy with employment and social obligations. Some seem to lose the determination to work at the goals they set for themselves to serve God with all their heart and soul and mind and strength. The Church of the Nazarene needs our Indian young people.

Many of these young people come to cities for work or just to get away. They get lost in these cities and are faced with many challenges. At home on the reservations, there was nothing to do. Now they must choose what to do. Pray for the missionaries who are going into the cities to try to help locate the lost ones for Christ.

God is at work among the Native Americans, but He has called us to do our part as well. May everyone who reads this book be challenged by God to be faithful in praying and in giving so that His kingdom may advance and His name may be glorified.